The Wild World of Animals

Hyenas

Hunters and Scavengers

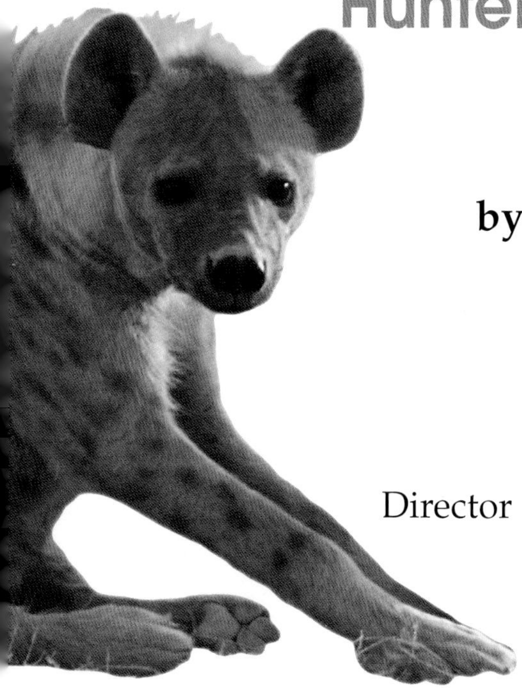

by Adele D. Richardson

Consultant:
Anne Warner
Director of Conservation and Education
The Oakland Zoo

Bridgestone Books
an imprint of Capstone Press
Mankato, Minnesota

Bridgestone Books are published by Capstone Press
151 Good Counsel Drive, P.O. Box 669, Mankato, Minnesota 56002
http://www.capstone-press.com

Library of Congress Cataloging-in-Publication Data
Richardson, Adele, 1966–
    Hyenas: hunters and scavengers/by Adele D. Richardson.
    p. cm.—(The wild world of animals)
    Includes bibliographical references (p. 24) and index.
    ISBN 0-7368-0963-5 *2876   4453 10/62*
    1. Hyenas—Juvenile literature. [1. Hyenas.] I. Title. II. Series.
QL737 .C24 R53 2002
599.74'3—dc21   00-012541

Summary: An introduction to hyenas describing their physical characteristics, habitat, young,
    food, predators, and relationship to people.

Editorial Credits
Erika Mikkelson, editor; Karen Risch, product planning editor; Linda Clavel, cover designer
    and illustrator; Heidi Schoof, photo researcher

Photo Credits
Corbis/Nigel J. Dennis, 20
Craig Brandt, 18
Index Stock Imagery, 1; Robert Franz, cover
Joe McDonald, 6
Pictor, 10
Richard Demler, 16
Tom & Pat Leeson, 8, 12
William Bernard, 4, 14

Table of Contents

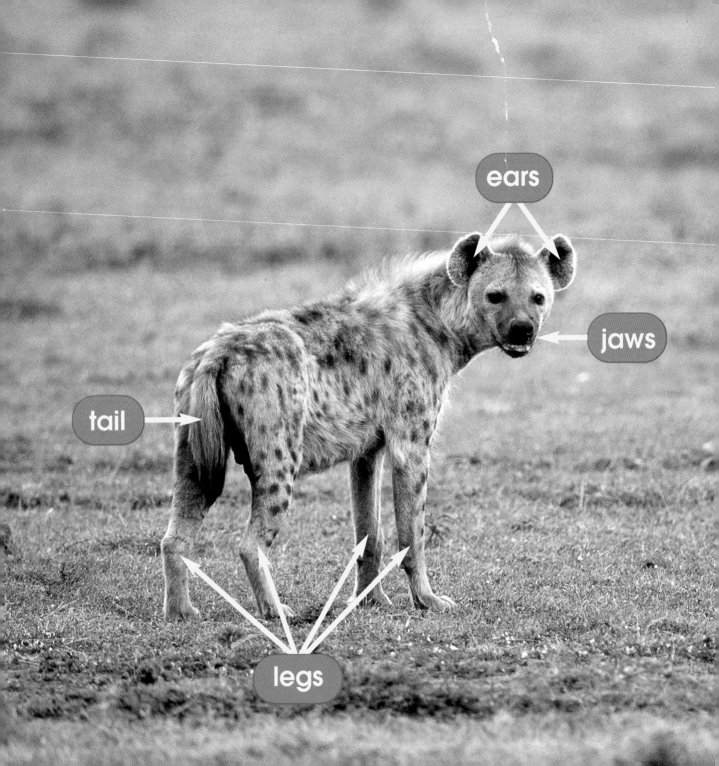

ears

jaws

tail

legs

Hyenas

Hyenas look like dogs. But a hyena's front legs are longer than its back legs. Hyenas use their powerful jaws to kill and eat animals. Hyenas hear well with their large, round ears.

Hyenas Are Mammals

Hyenas are mammals. Mammals are warm-blooded. Female mammals feed milk to their young. Mammals have hair or fur on their bodies. Most hyenas have red-brown or tan fur with dark spots.

warm-blooded

having a body temperature that stays the same

A Hyena's Habitat

Hyenas live in Africa. Most hyenas live in habitats with open grasslands. They easily find food on the open, grassy land. Hyenas sometimes live in rocky places.

habitat
the place where an animal lives

What Do Hyenas Eat?

Hyenas are carnivores. A carnivore eats only meat. Hyenas often eat livestock, wildebeests, and zebras. Hyenas mostly hunt together at night. They eat all parts of an animal they kill, including the bones and fur. Hyenas also will eat animal waste.

wildebeest

an African antelope that has a head like an ox and curved horns

11

Hyenas often make their homes in underground dens that are deserted by other animals.

Mating and Birth

Male and female hyenas can mate at any time during the year. Two young hyenas are born three to four months later. Young hyenas are born in dens.

mate
to join together to produce young

Hyena cubs drink milk from their mothers for 12 to 16 months. This is longer than any other meat-eating mammal.

Hyena Cubs

Young hyenas are cubs. Cubs weigh about 3 pounds (1.4 kilograms) at birth. Hyena cubs are born with black fur. Their fur begins to get spots when they are one and a half months old. Hyenas are the only animals born with teeth.

Predators

Hyenas are predators. They hunt and kill other animals. Few animals kill hyenas. Hyenas sometimes attack each other. Hyenas have their own territory. This area of land is where a hyena lives. Hyenas sometimes kill other hyenas that come into their territory.

FUN FACTS

Three kinds of hyenas live in the world. They are the spotted hyena, the brown hyena, and the striped hyena.

Laughing Hyenas

Hyenas use loud calls to send messages to each other. These calls can be growls, cackles, and rumbles. The spotted hyena sometimes is called the laughing hyena. Its call sounds like a person laughing. Spotted hyenas make this call when they are nervous or upset.

Hyenas and People

Hyenas and people do not get along. Hyenas attack livestock. Farmers often kill hyenas that come near their land. Some hyenas live near villages in Africa. They scavenge through people's garbage. Many people are afraid of hyenas.

scavenge
to search through garbage for food

Hands On: Hunting Hyena Tag

Hyenas need good hearing to hunt their prey. This game will show you how using your ears can help you capture your "prey."

What You Need

Several players
Blindfold or scarf
A large room

What You Do

1. Choose one player to be the hyena. Cover the player's eyes with the blindfold or scarf. This person sits in the middle of the room.
2. The rest of the players go to different areas of the room. One at a time, each of the players makes a noise. They might whistle, clap their hands, or stomp their feet.
3. Every time the hyena hears a noise, he or she points in the direction it came from. If the hyena points at the player who made the sound, that person becomes the hyena.
4. The players move to different places in the room when a new hyena is chosen. The game starts over.

Words to Know

carnivore (KAR-nuh-vor)—an animal that eats only meat

mammal (MAM-uhl)—a warm-blooded animal that has a backbone; female mammals feed milk to their young.

mate (MATE)—to join together to produce young; male and female hyenas mate to produce hyena cubs.

predator (PRED-uh-tur)—an animal that hunts and eats other animals

scavenge (SKAV-uhnj)—to search through garbage for food

territory (TER-uh-tor-ee)—an area of land that animals claim as their own to live in

Read More

Holmes, Kevin J. *Hyenas.* Animals. Mankato, Minn.: Bridgestone Books, 1999.

Rothaus, Don P. *Hyenas.* Plymouth, Minn.: Child's World, 1996.

Internet Sites

Animals A-Z: Hyena
http://www.oaklandzoo.org/atoz/azhyena.html
Animal Bytes: Spotted Hyena
http://www.seaworld.org/animal_bytes/hyenaab.html
Hyena
http://www.awf.org/wildlives/141
Spotted Hyena
http://www.sazoo-aq.org/hyena.html

Index